Wash Your Hands

By Sylvie Bright

Jungle Giggles

Wash Your Hands

Author: Sylvie Bright

Illustrator: Kristian Andreev

Copyright © 2018 Sylvie Bright

sylviebright.books@gmail.com

All rights reserved.

This book or any portion thereof many not be reproduced or used in any manner whatsoever without the express written permission of the author, except for the use of brief quotations in a book review.

ISBN: 978-0-9998481-0-4

The sun was setting in Jungleville. In front of Sam's house, the kids were still giggling and playing funny games.

"Sam, dinner's ready!" called Sam's mom.

The little tiger was very hungry.

"I have to go," Sam said to his friends while waving goodbye.

He rushed home, curious about what was for dinner. The smell was delicious! His family was already around the table, and Sam quickly took his seat as well. He didn't want everyone to have to wait for him.

Sam was just about to touch his food when he heard some weird, tiny voices chattering.

He looked around, but he couldn't see anyone talking.

Sam looked under his chair, but nobody was there. He looked under the table, but he still couldn't find anything unusual.

Sam scratched his head as he wondered where the sound was coming from. He focused on the voices.

There was a conversation going on.

"Everyone get ready! We'll wait for him to touch his food, and then we'll get inside his mouth. Then it will be easy! We'll spread around his body, and we'll make him sick in no time!"

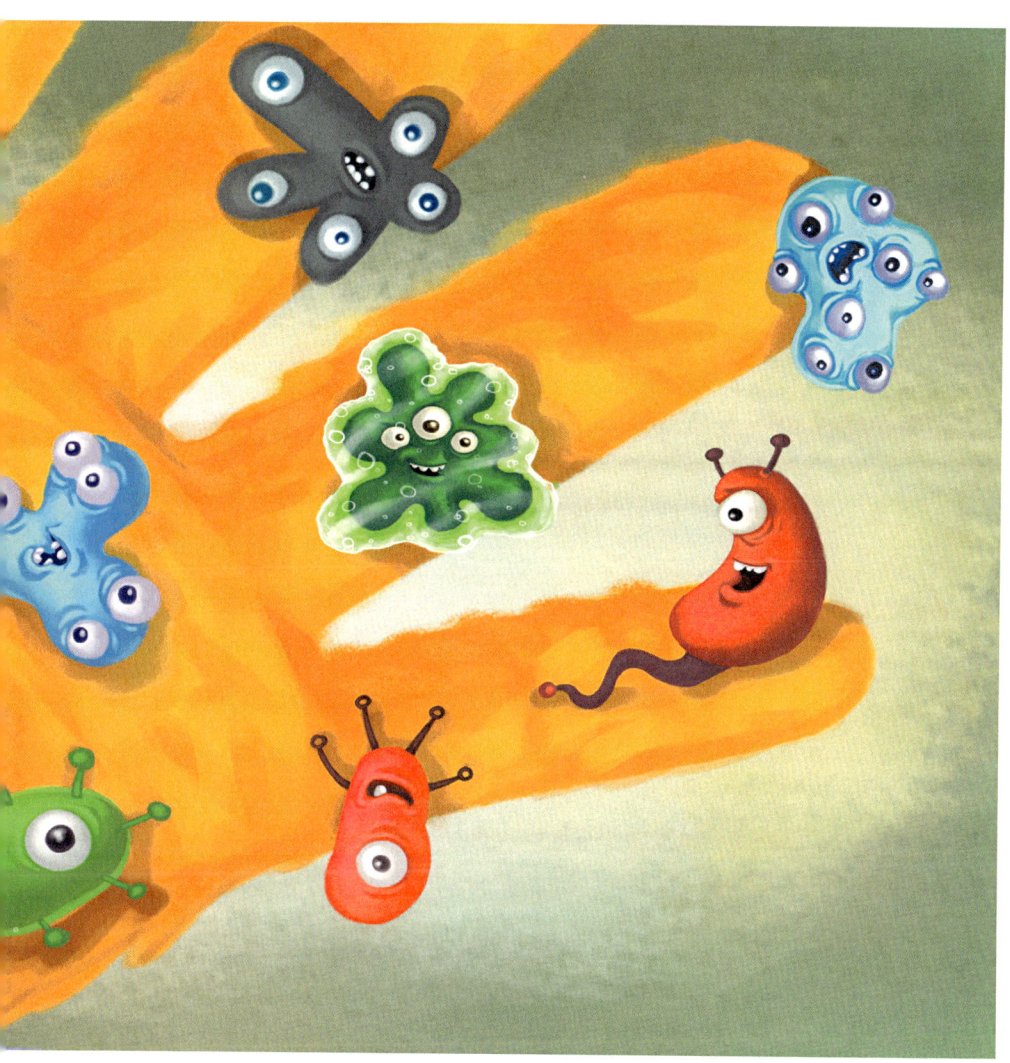

Sam couldn't see them, but there was a crowd of horrible tiny creatures planning their attack. Some had many legs; others didn't have legs at all. Some had many eyes and weird, funny colors. Their spotty bodies were all sleazy and gooey.

"I will make him cough," said a green creature with three eyes.

"I will make his tummy ache," threatened a red one with a long tail.

"I will make his throat sore," said a pink one with very red lips.

"We will make his nose run," added a group of tiny blue creatures that looked like worms.

Sam was scared. He couldn't see the creatures, but he definitely didn't like their plan. He didn't want to get sick! What could he do?

"Sam, did you wash your paws?" asked Mom suddenly. "I can hear the germs on your paws talking."

"You can hear them?!" cried Sam, astonished.

"We can all hear the germs, Sam," said Dad.

"Tigers have very strong hearing, and we can even hear the conversations of the tiniest creatures in the world," continued Dad.

"Like ants?" asked Sam.

"Even better! Like the GERMS," answered Dad.

"But what are the *germs*?" Sam asked. He still looked puzzled.

"Germs are like super small bugs. We can't see them. We have to use a special instrument called a *microscope* to see them. Germs are sneaky. They can make us sick if we allow them into our bodies."

"I want to get rid of them!" shouted Sam in disgust, jumping off his chair. "Get them off me! How do I get them off me?!?"

"Just wash your paws, Sam!" said Mom with a smile.

"If you want to be sure that they're all gone, count to 20, or say the alphabet while you're washing. That way, you'll know there's enough time for the soap to wash away all the germs," added Mom while Sam was running to the bathroom sink.

"Do I hear the water running?!" Sam heard an upset voice coming from his hands. It was one of the germs.

"Do I smell soap?!" cried another germ.

"1 2 3 4 5 6 7 8 9 10 11 . . .," Sam counted while washing his hands.

"Nooo! Nooo! Nooo!" cried the ugly minions as they washed down the drain with the soapy water.

The germs' evil plan was not going to work!

Sam was happy. He could finally enjoy his dinner safe from germs.

The next day at school, Sam decided to go on a rescue mission. He put on his "Super Sam" t-shirt so he could feel like a hero. His mom's red scarf made a perfect cape. Super Sam spent all morning talking to his friends about the germs.

"We must ALWAYS wash our hands before eating, and we will be safe! Playing, cuddling with our pets, going to the toilet, sneezing, and coughing bring lots of germs onto our hands, but there's nothing to be afraid if you wash with soap," explained Sam.

Super Sam had so many kids to rescue from the germs.

It was time for lunch, and the voices of the germs were not to be heard anywhere around the room. Sam was happy. His mission was a success.

As he was preparing to eat, Sam heard a single tiny voice coming from somewhere in the middle of the hall.

"I can do this by myself! I will make him sick! There is still hope . . ."

Sam listened carefully to find where the sound was coming from. Finally, he got it! It was coming from Liam the monkey. Liam was about to put a piece of banana in his mouth. His hands were really dirty.

Sam was fast as a rocket! He got up from his seat, jumped over the monkey, and grabbed the banana.

"There is a germ on your hands, Liam!" Sam explained to his friend. "Did you wash your hands?"

"Oh, no, I forgot!" answered the surprised monkey.

"Thank you for saving me, Sam!" said Liam after coming back from washing his hands. "You really are our Super Sam!"

"You're welcome, Liam!" Sam said happily as he went back to his seat.

It was going to be another wonderful day in Jungleville.

Ask your child:

- What do germs do to you?
- Why did Sam wash his hands?
- How did Sam wash his hands to be sure that he got rid of the germs?
- Why do you think Sam wanted to save all his friends from the germs?
- Where do you think you can find a lot of germs at home? What about at school?
- When do we need to wash our hands?

Made in the USA
Lexington, KY
11 October 2018